RITA ANN HIGGINS

GODDESS ON THE
MERVUE BUS

SALMON  POETRY

First published in 1986 by
SalmonPublishing, Galway,

This edition by Salmon Publishing Ltd in 1993
A division of Poolbeg Enterprises Ltd,
Knocksedan House,
Swords, Co. Dublin, Ireland.

**Salmon Publishing Ltd receives financial assistance from
the Arts Council/An Chomhairle Ealaíon.**

A catalogue record for this book is available from the British Library.

ISBN 1 897648 09 X

Cover photograph by Gillian Buckley
Cover design by Poolbeg Group Services Ltd
Set by Mac Book Limited
Printed by The Guernsey Press Limited,
Vale, Guernsey, Channel Islands.

For Christy, Heather, Jennifer

and the rent man

ACKNOWLEDGEMENTS

Some of these poems have appeared in *The Salmon, Writing in the West, Cyphers, Outlet, Criterion, Broadsheet 1, Folio International, Echo Room, Honest Ulsterman, Quarto, Midland Review* (USA), and *Oklahoma State Review*. 'The Day Bridie O'Flaherty was made Mayor' was broadcast by RTE's 'Good Morning Ireland.' A number of the poems have been dramatised by the Galway Theatre Workshop (Women in the Ordinary).

◆◆◆

Contents

Women sit or move to and fro, some old, some young.
The young are beautiful, but the old are more beautiful than the young.

Walt Whitman

Consumptive in the Library

About you:
you carry a kidney donor card,
not yet filled in,
a St. Christopher's round your neck
on a brown shoe lace,
(to ward off demons and politicians),
memories of Sweet Afton,
the racing page from the *Daily Express*
and an unsociable cough.

About me:
I carry illusions
of becoming a famous poet,
guilt about that one time in Baltinglass,
fear that the lift will stop at Limbo,
a slight touch of sciatica
plus an anthology of the Ulster poets.

Unlike your peers
you will not take warmth
from cold churches or soup kitchens,
instead, for long periods, you will
exasperate would-be poets with illusions,
in the reference room of the Galway County Library.

I started with Heaney,
you started to cough.
You coughed all the way to Ormbsy,
I was on the verge of Mahon.

Daunted, I left you the Ulster Poets
to consume or cough at.

I moved to the medical section.

Evangeline

Evangeline,
God help her,
reacts to macho men,
who in the end
expect her to survive
on the draught
of far-flung embraces,

not interested in
her food-mixer
philosophies,
her many ways
with crux pastry.

Only wanting
what she can never
give freely.

Look Evan, through
your stainless net curtains,
another far-flung embrace—
take it,

opium for the dead
self that leads
to seven second security.

She had notions,
some dreary Tuesdays,
about swish red
sports cars
and a villa
off the something
coast of France.

She saw herself
in a plunging neckline,
offering her condolences
to Anthony Quinn
Lee Marvin types.

Much later
that same lifetime,
when the kids are asleep,
she crawls out
of her apron pocket
and meets herself
for the first time that day
in the eyes of Martha Glynn,
ten Silk Cut
and a small white sliced.

'Will we see you
on the bingo bus
a Friday, Martha G?'

'I wouldn't miss it
for the world.'
And out of her mouth
came all the eights,
and she brought laughter
to all in Folan's shop
for the second
time this month.

The Day Bridie O'Flaherty was made Mayor

(for Jennifer)

Your sister was upstairs
chanting to god Springsteen
on the headphones.

Your father
was in the Labour Exchange
waiting for the statues to move.

Your ageing mother
was watching four dead mackerel
on the draining-board,
hoping they would fillet themselves.

And you my love
were cutting grass
with the new scissors
we got free from Family Album
with your father's moccasins
that were never paid for.

And the dollar swerved two point two cents shy of the pound

Mrs. McEttigan

No coincidence was this,
it was arranged by God,
you would say.

Me, posting a letter.
You, you were just there.

You, from somewhere in Ulster,
I loved your accent.
Me, from somewhere in space,
you loved my mother.

You always said the same thing
'Your mother is in Heaven,
she was a saint, God be good to her.'

You lifted your eyes.

You, with the posh brooch,
two stones missing, your Mass hat.

I was just there.

Don't ever die, Mrs. McEttigan,
I need to see you outside the Post Office
sending glances to a saint.

Tommy's Wife

She wasn't always this bitter,
I knew her when she sang in pubs.

She was younger then and free,
a happy life she spent.

Working in Woolworths,
she kept herself well. Blue eye shadow.

She married for the sake of the kid.
A lot of envelopes she received. The day.

It started out well for her
the family stood by her then.

Tommy looks strong, many friends,
likes Guinness, sex and unemployment.

She lost blue eye shadow first year,
Sara now five months, teething hard.

She didn't sing in pubs anymore,
she wasn't as friendly as before.

The other three children didn't delay,
she remembered wearing blue eye shadow.

The coal man hated calling now,
he didn't understand her anger.

Tommy looks strong, many friends,
likes Guinness, sex and unemployment.

Unnecessary Work

(for Bernie)

Sunday evening
we walked
unwanted calories
into the prom
for leisure.

Our duty now
homeward-bound
to visit the mother's grave.

On an unkempt plot nearby
a community of pink carnations
overpowers me.

'You won't have luck for it,'
my sister said.

Later on they stood
in a black Chinese vase
accompanied by
one blooming spike
of white gladiolus
the cat had broken off.

Their agreeable essence
adds life to this room.

I mime a hurried
prayer for the repose
of the soul of
Mary Elizabeth Cooke.

What is a Canary?

Hippolyta O'Hara
would like to own
a mare called Bella.

But where would she keep her,
she lives in a housing estate,
no mares named Bella allowed.

Hippolyta O'Hara
would like to own
a minotaur called Harry.

But where would she keep him,
she lives in a housing estate,
no minotaurs named Harry allowed.

Hippolyta O'Hara
would like to own
a crocodile called Leonard.

But where would she keep him,
she lives in a housing estate,
no crocodiles named Leonard allowed.

Hippolyta O'Hara
would like to own
a canary called Dominico,
but the cat would eat him.

What about the housing estate?

A canary is a canary
in a housing estate
or in a bishop's house.

The cat is the problem.

Work On

Nostalgia takes me back—
the shirt factory toilet.

Where country girls met
and sucked cigarette ends on Monday mornings.

Sunday night was discussed, the Ranch House,
his acreage, physique and the make of his car.

Precisely they swayed to and fro,
tannoy blasted sweet lyrics, their hero.

Two jived to the beat, two killed the smoke
and seven sank further into hand-basins.

Boisterous laughter echoed and betrayed lost time.
'Back to work girls,' supervisor sang.

A thousand buttonholes today.
A thousand Ranch House fantasies the weekend.

Work On.

The Apprentices

Daily they perch
during factory lunchtimes
on their man-made Olympus.

Who will attempt to pass
through their veil of lust unscathed
by Henry Leech-along's recital
of his nine favourite adjectives?

Hardly the unprotected townie
shielded only by the active ingredients
of a lifetime's venial sins.

Maybe some young one from the Tech.,
the brazen Bridget variety—
mother in a home,
father in a bottle.

Hey you! Wearers of brown acrylic pullovers,
a yellow stripe across your chest-bone
means your mother is still alive,
think not of other people's undertones,
of milk-white flesh, of touching thighs.

AnCo never trained you for this.

Stay awhile, Pavlovian pets, fill your sights
with more ambitious things,
like when your apprenticeship ends
and you are released on the world
a qualified this or that.

Right now you are an apprentice's echo,
know your station.

The Syrup of Longevity

'Awful about poor Mr. Carney,
only fifty,
wife and ten kids left behind.
Plenty of exercise and a good
clean diet that's what we need.'

'Don't gimme no tripe about them
Air Rubex, my own father
lived to be ninety
not a day's labour in him.
No single day passed that
he didn't colour his egg with
a generous teaspoon of salt.
If his mutton stew didn't have
at least four inches of grease
relaxing on top of it
he wouldn't put a tooth in it.
He'd take ash from a dead man's lips,
he drank poteen every day of his life.
The day before he died
he sat up in the bed and had a working-man's
helping of mutton stew.
His mind went years ago
but that's neither here or there,
didn't he live to see nicely?'

Annaghmakerrig

At Annaghmakerrig in the semi-dark
you might see things moving
in the trees
if you didn't have your wits akimbo.

Once in a dream I saw Tyrone Guthrie,
in his good suit, fishing green sausages
out of the duck pond.

I tried hard not to see
the four grisly ghouls lashing
the seven swinging cats with their bad breath.

The little black demon with no arse
was not really there at all
nor did he devour six toasted mice
dipped in aubergine sauce.

It's an absolute lie to say
that five truncated gobelinus
did the two-hand-reel in the foyer
each evening before dinner.

I didn't sleep well at Annaghmakerrig.

Power Cut

Black-out excitement, enchanting,
chasing shadows up and down.

Delirious children play scary
monsters, the walls laugh back.

Father bear sleeps it off,
dreams of good westerns.

Mother bear thinks it cultural,
collects young, reads by candle shade.

Siblings content, maternal wing snug,
drifting softly, land of mild and honey.

Father bear slept enough, weary of culture,
'Try the lights upstairs,' he shouts.

Mother bear switches on. Another culture shock,
westerns, yoghurt and the late news.

Poetry Doesn't Pay

People keep telling me
Your poems, you know,
you've really got something there,
I mean really.

When the rent man calls, I go
down on my knees, and through
the conscience box I tell him,

'This is somebody speaking,
short distance, did you know
I have something here with my poems?
People keep telling me.'

'All I want is fourteen pounds
and ten pence, hold the poesy.'

'But don't you realise
I've got something here.'

'If you don't come across
with fourteen pounds and ten pence soon
you'll have something at the side of the road,
made colourful by a little snow.'

'But.'

'But nothing,
you can't pay me in poems or prayers
or with your husband's jokes,
or with photographs of your children
in lucky lemon sweaters
hand-made by your dead grand aunt
who had amnesia and the croup.

'I'm from the Corporation,
what do we know or care about poesy,
much less grand amnostic dead aunts.'

'But people keep telling me.'

'They lie.

'If you don't have fourteen pounds
and ten pence, you have nothing
but the light of the penurious moon.'

It's About Time

One day a car pulled up,
the driver asked me the way to Tuam.

I replied,
'Sir, do you know
that where Tuam was yesterday it no longer is today.'

The following day a car pulled up,
the driver asked me, 'Was there a way to Tuam?'

I replied,
'Sir, do you not know that where Tuam was yesterday
it can no longer be today.'

On the third day a car pulled up,
the driver asked me, 'Where are you today?'

'Sir,' I said,
'Today I am in Tuam and it is four minutes to
midnight.'

'Madam,' said he,
'You've got the right time, but you're in the wrong
place'

Goddess on the Mervue Bus

Aphrodite
of the homely bungalow,
cross curtains,
off-white Anglia at the side.

Your father
(who is no Zeus)
turns old scrap
into rolled gold
nightly from memory,

looks down on you
from his scrap mountain,
hurling forks of caution
about the tin-can man

who fumbles in the aisle
of the Mervue bus,
longing for the chance
of a throwaway smile,
a discarded bus ticket.

O Goddess on the Mervue bus,
no scrap dealer fashioned
you from memory or want,
you were spun from golden
dust, a dash of dream.

Enslaver of mortals,
you choose me.

Once when you yawned
I saw myself
sitting cross-legged
on a lonely molar
waiting for the crunch.

Lizzie Kavanagh

There's nothing wrong
with Lizzie Kavanagh,
'Kavvy' for short,
she has that coat
for ages.

It's maroon imitation fur,
extras include
one leatherette belt.

When it was new
she only wore it
to her mother's
and Quinnsworth.

Now she wears it
everywhere, she says
it brings her luck,
once she didn't have
it on at bingo and
'Never Been Kissed'
was called and she
only needed one number
for a full house,
after that she swore—

it was definitely the coat.

There's a comfortable
depression on the seat
of it from travelling
on the Shantalla bus
to see her sister-in-law.

She says she'd be lost
without Aggie—
that's her sister-in-law,
and mother—
that's her mother.

There's nothing wrong
with Lizzie Kavanagh,
she just likes bingo,
her mother, Aggie—
that's her sister-in-law,
and maroon imitation—
that's her coat.

Secrets

Secrets are for keeping
not for hiding,
the spines of wardrobes
will talk, sooner or later.

Keep your secrets in your heart,
in hip joints,
between folds of flesh,
or under rotting ulcers.

Never tell best friends,
in time their minds will leak
from old age or too much whiskey.

Don't succumb to pleas of
'I swear I'll never tell,'
eleven will know within the hour.

Don't ever tell priests.

Keep well clear of burning bushes,
investigative mothers-in-law
with egg-shell slippers
and Dundee cake.

Never tell the living dead.

Be on the look-out
for lean neighbours
who slither between hedges
and pose as anteaters.

They're really secret stealers in disguise.

As for keeping a diary,
when you're gone
for entertainment, on wet days
and after funerals,
your nearest and dearest
will read it aloud with relish.

Try blushing with clay between your teeth.

The Test

Iquanidae Londis,
a witch doctor with the Regional,
she loves her job.
Her credentials she keeps
where her heart used to be,
it reads 'Gut Snipper'.
A vocation for it you might say,
if you had the guts left.

I sampled the test once,
the event I hid deep in the layers of my liver.
One scarred afternoon two years wiser
I collided with witch doctor,
one look into her mad scarlet eyes
brought the whole event nearer the floor.

'Listen,' she said, 'there's nothing to it,
I just ram this little off-white tube
forcibly down your stingy little oesophagus,
wriggle it around awhile,
say forty-five mins multiplied by five.'

'There's a small, sharp, well-dressed blade
at the top of it,
as soon as it attaches itself to your shapely
virginal gut and I see that it's got a piece
of you between its teeth,

I'll just give a little tug with all my sincerity
and up she'll come with gut in hand, hopefully.
Or else we'll have to go again.'

So we went again, and on the seventh day I enquired.

'Am I or am I not?'

'Listen, medical card number 64279,
you are no coeliac
but you have the loveliest looking
large intestine I've ever had fourteen snips of.
Go forth and be proud.'

All Buckled Up in the Industrial Estate

Count them buckles,
stack them high.

In rows of boredom
the mind drips,
esteem leaks
all the way
to your fag packet.

We count in rivers and riddles,
we smoke our own.

(Midday Chant)
     Count them buckles
     stack them high
     make them beauties scrape the sky.
(End of Chant)

Time out for lunch and human behaviour.
Thirty minutes of darkness to buckle down.

'What have you?'
'Easy singles.'
'Are you easy?'
'I'm simple.'
'Me too.'

'Who do you want to be when you grow down?'
'A banjaxed buckle.'

'Me too.'

Lotus Eater from Bohermore

Death is the end of life: ah! why
Should life all labour be?   Lord Tennyson

Salmon-ways of life hold little scenery
for this ageing man in search of employment;
sit-about on an oil rig, his fantasy—
but the rig would have to come to Mohammed
c/o Silver Dollar Amusement Arcade.

Badly in need of a pocket watch,
his mottoes etched on an empty wallet.
No sign of the crock of gold—
it would be the wrong currency anyway.

His swollen brains exhausted
with fantasies of the big break—
nearly always it's an arm or a leg,
never the winning grin
of the Pakistani dealer on the blackjack table.

Philosophies he could sell you,
his dreams he gives away,
but never his place in the dole queue—
it's his security, a high price to pay.

The German for Stomach

(for Eva)

I was waiting for the twenty-past
in the rain, trying to think
of the German for stomach.

While I was racking,
I took time out for
a stew fantasy.
When a blue Merc pulled
out in front of a brown Mini,
I had stew fantasy interruptus.

The man in the brown Mini
was blue and furious
but he didn't let on.
Poor Rex later that day.

The blue Merc made me think
of blue skies and blue seas,
then it came to me.
Bauch, that's it, der Bauch.
I said to myself all the way home,
except when I passed the graveyard,
time for another stew fantasy.

I got off near Kane's butchers.
Inside they were discussing
the gimp and colour of Sean Sweeney's
duodenum when the doctor opened him.
They called it the Northern Province.

It was on the tip of my tongue
and out it tumbled.
'Bauch is the German for stomach.'

His wife said,
'Are you sure you don't want
a carrier bag for that, loveen?'

I could see that
the butcher was overwhelmed,
he wanted to shout
Lapis Lazuli, Lapis Lazuli,
but instead he said,

'You wouldn't put a dog out in it.'

Almost Communication

My father just passed me
in his Fiat 127
I was cycling my bicycle 'Hideous'.

They stopped at O'Meara's
for the *Connacht Tribune*.
As I passed I shouted
'road hog' in the window.

The occupants laughed.

Before this he owned
a Renault 12,
we called it the
'Ballyhaunis cow killer'.

Later we met outside the sister's,
'Wouldn't you think
he'd buy you a decent bike, the miser.'

'If he had your money,' I said
and we laughed.

The neighbours with their ears
to the rose bushes
think that we're great friends.

I haven't seen his eyes for years.

The Benevolent Coat Saver in Black

(for Angela Small)

In the doorway of our shop this ebon nun
declared it, 'Something to save my good coat.

The size doesn't matter but the colour, yes,
it must be a dark shade of black.

This seems adequate, but yellow,
it won't match the colour of my faith.

My faith is black as black as a crow,
I'm saving my good coat. Did I mention?

This, a bit smockish, too wide,
much room for secrets, not allowed.'

'It suits you grand,
blends in darkly with your glance,

It's yours for a prayer, will you have it?'
'No it's the wrong colour black.'

'You have a merciful back to save your good coat,
will you save mine as well?'

Middle-aged Irish Mothers

Germinating sopranos in conservative head squares
are the middle-aged Irish mothers in heavy plaid
coats, who loiter after Mass in churches,

> Lord make me an instrument of your peace;
> Where there is hatred, let me sow love;

to light candles for the Joes and Tommies of the
                                    drinking world,
the no-hopers, that they might pack it in,
if it's the will of God,

> Where there is injury, pardon;
> Where there is discord, union;

to pray for Susan's safe delivery, Bartley's gambling,
Mrs. Murray's veins, that they would not bother her
so much, not forgetting Uncle Matt's shingles.

> Where there is doubt, faith;
> Where there is despair, hope;

Soon, not out of boredom, they will move diagonally
through their cruciform sanctuary to do the Stations
in echoing semi-song whispers,

We adore thee O Christ we bless thee,
 because by thy cross thou hast redeemed the
                                                 world

sincere pleas to dear Jesus, that the eldest might
get off with a light sentence, pledges of no more
                                        smoking,
and guarantees of attendance at the nine Fridays,

Where there is darkness, light;
Where there is sadness, joy;

finally, for the Pope's intentions, Mr Glynn's
                                brother-in-law,
the sweeps ticket that it might come up,
                        but only if it's the will of God,

O Sacred Heart of Jesus, I place
all my trust and confidence in thee.

I like these middle-aged Irish mothers, in heavy
                                plaid coats,
one of them birthed me on the eve of a saint's
                                feast day,
with a little help from Jesus and his Sacred Heart.

I tell you most solemnly, anything you ask for
from the Father he will grant in my name.

Ode to Rahoon Flats

O Rahoon, who made you
to break the hearts
of young girls with
pregnant dreams

of an end terrace,
crisp white clothes
lines and hire purchase
personalities?

You don't care if her
children crawl into her
curved spine,
distort her thinking.

You put Valium on a
velvet cushion
in the form of a
juicy red apple.

Rahoon, why are you
so cruel to young
husbands, hooked on
your butter voucher

bribes? If you crumbled

would it take three days
or would the ground swallow
you up, payment for your sins?

Old Friend

Upstairs in Powell's our chance encounter,
it must have been fifteen years.

Today made her old, she trembled here.
Outside, the sun made flesh in cars uncomfortable.

On hay-making summers gone by her slow words,
reminiscing,
'We worked you hard and you only a nipper.

And how's Carmel? I remember the day she was
christened,
I cycled four miles in the rain.'

She was my mother's best friend, 'a good neighbour'
echoed in that inner distance where the veins began.

Her black mantilla was too tight,
she didn't seem to mind, he was worth it.

'It was my younger brother,
at seventy he was taken. Cancer,' she whispered.

She gave a pound to the children to share,
'Your husband's hair is lovely.'

An old tear trickled and we almost hugged,
'I'll see you again, please God.'

She Never Heard of Cromwell

When I worked there
I thought she knew everything.

When she walked
her buttocks screamed,

'I know everything.'

Years later I came back.

'I'll have a sly coffee
behind a newspaper and
a slice of your best
wisdom, well done.'

A patron asked for
Chicken Maryland,
and who was Cromwell?

Years later
when she returned
from Maryland, she said,

'I never heard of Cromwell,
all meals are served with chipped potatoes.'

Seventeen Times Upon a Time for You

(for Heather)

'Tell me about
the stolen
canes from
Briar Hill
school.'

You want
to empty me
of stolen cane
catastrophes.
'Again,' you said.

I told you
who did it,
who his mother was,
her teeth count,
site of the family plot,
place of the
family pew.

I told you
Shady Kelly
got the blame
because his hair
was white,

grown-ups called him
Al Somebody.

I gave you
dates, minutes,
hours, years,
sweat, blood,
false enthusiasm,
sincere grief.
I took off
his accent
his mother's smile.

I exaggerated
a little
when I
banged my head
off the wall.

I lied
a little
about his
brother,
the priest,
about his
poker,
pill and drink
problem.

I took off

his speech
impediment,
the way
his aunt walks.

I put life
into the
lifelessness
for you.
I put flesh
on friendly
skeletons
for you.

I was weary
from you.
I pulled
out a nerve
ending from me.

I took
a deep breath,
my leave of you.
You were asleep.

Not true.
'Again,' you said.

The Long Ward

I have never seen
an old woman
eating an orange.

The long ward
for the old
and sometimes
the odd appendix.

The long ward
for craic,
for prayer,
a joke, a song
and sometimes pain.

In the long ward
Silvermints are
shared and returned
with photographs of
'My second eldest'
or 'This one is in Canada.'

Some come to visit,
to care, to love,
few to count acres
in old women's eyes.

In the long ward
it pleases when
the priest passes
your bed.

In the dead of night
a cry for somebody's son.
No welcome for the grey
box that comes to call.

Thin legs you see,
smiling mothers
in new Dunnes dressing gowns,
new slippers,
boxes of tissues
they would never use at home.

Always one to joke
about the black doctor,
always one to complain
about the cold tea, no ham.

An eye on the clock,
a hand on the rosary beads,
pain well out of sight.

The loved grandchildren
embrace good-looking oranges
and ancient smiles.

God-of-the-Hatch Man

(for Community Welfare Officers everywhere)

Smoking and yes mamming,
snoozing in the fright
of his altered expression,
caused always by the afternoon.

Tepid water sipper, coffee glutton,
pencil pointer, negative nouner,
God-of-the-hatch man, hole in the wall.

We call religiously every Thursday,
like visiting the holy well,
only this well purports to give you things
instead of taking them away.

Things like scarlatina, schizophrenia,
migraine, hisgraine but never your grain,
lockjaw and wind, silicosis,
water on the knee, hunger in the walletness.

We queue for an hour or three,
we love to do this,
our idea of pleasure,
Then whatever-past what-past he likes,
he appears.

Tepid water sipper, coffee glutton,
pencil pointer, negative nouner,
God-of-the-hatch man, hole in the wall.

He gives us money and abuse,
the money has a price,
the abuse is free.

'Are you sure your husband isn't working?'
'Are you sure grumbling granny is quite dead?'
'Are you sure you're not claiming for de Valera?'
'Are you sure you count six heads in every bed?'

Hummer of Andy Williams' tunes,
most talked about man in the waiting room,
tapper of the pencil on the big brown desk.

God-of-the-hatch man, hole in the wall.
God-of-the-hatch man, hole in the wall.

Mona

Mona doesn't die here
anymore, she lives
in a house at the back
of her mind.

Some place small,
cosy and warm,
fully detached,
a single storey,
with no gable ending,
a high wall
but no door.

Away from
tenants' associations,
rent man's,
poor man's,
light bills,
heavy bills,
free newspapers,
and six-year-old perpetrators on skates.

When she was here
she was afraid
of salutations,
candied appreciations,

of tendon squeezing
politicians
who didn't care.

In supermarkets
she was tricked by
pennies off here,
free holidays over there,
buy three and get
anxiety for nothing.

She was a coupon saver,
she saved them
but they never saved her.

Mona doesn't die there
anymore, she lives
in a shed at the back
of her house.

Some place small,
cosy and warm,
a high wall
but no door.

Sunny Side Plucked

We met outside
the seconds chicken
van at the market.

He was very American,
I was very married.

We chatted about
the home-made marmalade
I bought two miles
from home.

He said the eggs were big,
I said he'd been eating
his carrots.

'Do you always buy
seconds chickens?'

'Only when I come late.'

The witch in me
wanted to scramble
his eggs.

The devil in him
wanted to pluck
my chicken.

We parted
with an agreement
written by the eyes.